COTTON

Cotton

Najya A. Williams

Printed in the United States of America

ISBN: 978-0-9992722-1-3

The BGM Press
Washington D.C. 20019
najyawilliams.com

COTTON

Table of Contents

Why *Cotton?*

"Cotton is a refreshing collection capturing both the essence and struggle of black womanhood but marrying these experiences with new and old age experiences of race. Williams' fluid but pointed words exude not just descriptions of experiences but the raw and in many cases unexposed feelings and emotions that accompany experiences of black womanhood and race. Any and all should pick up this read to not only reminisce and find a speckle of oneself sewn in each page, but also to experience and participate in the raw and needed exposure of blackness, womanhood and plain old life and how this impacts mental wellness and healthiness. A must read for all!"

Lauren Carson, Executive Director/Founder Black Girls Smile Inc.

"Your poetry is all at the same time astonishingly truthful, gritty, and uplifting. While I was moved to tears at some passages, the clear message of exhorting one to be their best selves was palpable.

Any person who wishes to read Cotton should be prepared to experience passion, confusion, desperation, anguish, and finally, determination — that the world can and should be an equal place for all people. What a thought provoking volume — I look forward to the day where your words inspire an entire generation of people to change the world!"

Linda Larson, The Economic Club of Washington, D.C.

"Let me start off by saying that even the highest expectations I had for this book were blown out of the water. This is amazing. I was so impressed by the way you easily and expertly switch between voices and characters. There were times when I could hear the Najya I know reading the poems out to me (even some of the ones I had never heard before). There were other times where you seamlessly and effortlessly transported me to a completely different time and place, and I felt like I was reading an excerpt from a journal or listening into a prayer."

Tatiana Patino, Harvard College

"This work [Cotton], as I'm sure you know, is beyond brilliant. Emanating from the pages [...], I can really feel the passion that runs through your mind when you're piecing these works together. But passion doesn't make good poetry. Your expert use of the English language and literary technique, combined with your passion and emotion, makes good poetry, and I'm blessed to have been able to have read it."

Hakeem Angulu, Harvard College

"This [Cotton] is a poignant collection of poetry that truly captures the experiences of Black Americans. Read it and be enlightened."

Pavita Singh, Editor, pavEDITa

"The way [Najya] pieces together words on paper to create a dance on your tongue and an ache in your heart is divine and one of a kind. How she found all the right words for this moment in time, I will never know. Read it [Cotton]. You will feel in your physical body a range of emotions you never knew you had, and know by the end of it, you will feel like you have found a sister. I have read and re-read, gifted, cried over, healed, and gleamed empathy through works from a very select group [of] women of color poets: Claudia Rankine, Rupi Kaur, Sarah Kay, and Warsan Shire. Today, to my delight, I have added [Najya] Williams to this group of incredible and unapologetic sisters."

Sarah Hsu, The Milken Scholars Program

"Choosing to act in the face of deadly assaults is not simply an act of will, as Najya Williams reminds us throughout this book [*Cotton*]. It requires a sense of community and affirmation, along with a deep grounding in history. With lines like "I imagine this is how my slave ancestors felt/Silenced/Rid of their tongue/Not because they didn't know how to fight/They felt trapped between saving their future children/ And keeping the living ones safe"– Williams weaves together past, present and future in a powerful call to celebrate and fight for the power and beauty of Black lives in America."

Dr. Phyllis Mentzell Ryder, Associate Professor of Writing, Director of Writing Center, The George Washington University

Author's Note

Family,

We are flesh born of flesh, yet still divine. Our parents' best and worst laced like poetry along our vertebrae. Our ancestors' prayers made human. Made soul. Made life. We are born of and into a community of power that has existed since the beginning of time. What a beautiful history to have!

Cotton is a collection of poetry that is a raw and honest window into my heart as an Afro-Caribbean woman living in today's society. With a heart for activism, it has been extremely difficult to stay current on what is happening in the United States, whether it's about the continued lack of clean water in Flint or the triggering murders of Black men across the country. It's even more difficult when I look at my family and friends, stained dark with melanin, kinky tresses on their heads, and lips fuller than life. A fear coils up my spine and takes my breath away each and every time I think about how my mother, my brothers, my sisters, any of my family could be the next viral hashtag. However, I don't stay locked in that place for long because I know I stand on strength, perseverance, and faith that is unparalleled. My ancestors did not survive the Middle Passage, slavery, Jim Crow, and blatant racism for me to buckle in the face of adversity. They did it so I'd have wind beneath my wings when I finally decided to fly.

It would be remiss of me to not identify some of the key voices that are not present in this collection: members of the LGBTQIA, Muslim, and immigrant communities. Your words are needed. Your words are power. Quite frankly, your words will stain many lives with the compassion, love, and hope this society so desperately needs. I stand at the intersection of womanhood, first-generation immigration, and Blackness, but it does not make me an expert on the "Black experience." I write my story and I respect the need for you to tell your own. Even though my lived experiences don't directly align with yours, and I can't expressly address them in this collection, know that I stand with you as a sister who empathizes and an ally who wants equality for all of us. As I keep you in my prayers, keep me in yours. We weren't brought this far into the fight to be left here.

We are flesh born of flesh, yet still divine. It is my hope that you find home, history, and a touch of that divinity in this collection.

Thank you for taking the time to read *Cotton*. Your time is precious and I couldn't have done it without you.

Najya

~

A hilarious woman once said:
"Mirror, mirror on the wall,
I am my mother after all."

Cotton is dedicated **to my mama, my BFF, my Queen**. If I
become half the woman and mother you are, I'll still be
above average.

Part I

What happened?

~

To understand the present and the
future, one must revisit the past.
Understand it. Get knee deep in it. It
may not be pretty. Even hard to digest,
but dear God, it's necessary. Don't run.
We are journeying together.

Before There Was, We Were

The dust settles around me
Disturbed by my newfound exuberance
Or is it really newfound
What these eyes can't see is the power that resonated long
before me
I am the fertile land
The silt that fertilizes these roadways we call blood vessels
I am the intellect
The variable that completes every square in this circle of life
I am the innovation
The sea vessel that keeps your feet above water
Even when my head is submerged beneath
My body contorts into magic
Leaving a sprinkle of me as a trail to be explored

I am the shackles
The metal cool against your flesh that stirs the passionate
freedom flickering in you
I am the submission
The meekness I suppress to keep subservience a distant
memory
I am the scars
The alarm clocks that will only stop ringing when you stop
sleeping in this tank of venom
I am the protest sign
The spirit thought to be dead but as alive as the strength
flowing in you
I am the mighty fist
The unity broken by the wills of this world
Piecing together the ideas of togetherness before this
recklessness consumes them

I am nonviolence
The slight whisper of greatness that ignites a fire so bright
You can almost hear it roaring through your flesh
Branding a fresh image of what speaking up means
I am the voting ballot
Allowing your ink to stain my senses and throw us into the
pit of change
Shaking the strings that weigh me down into the abyss of
dull conservatism
I am the White House
The leader so desperately needed when everything else
escapes into the dark of the night
I am the President
The King of my castle when society attempts to wrangle me
to my Queendom

Before there was an inkling of the doubt in the curves of
my plains
The coloring that seeps into my skin
The shapes put together to sculpt my face
The fear of finding out the secrets of my blood
The complacency adapted in this new home
Before there was the doubt that I'd forget every link in my
DNA
Every drop of wisdom I sought in nature
Before there was, I was magnificent
I was pretty
Glowing
Priceless
Sought
I was wanted
I was so that I could stretch beneath my community

My back now a raft to stay afloat in the suffocating sea of
this moment

Before there was anything, I was
Before there was, I was and you were
We were
We are and still are the power we all seek
Step up and embrace your talent
Before there was, we were
Royal
Trumpets will blare from the foyer of my palace
Each and every day
Because I was, am, and always will be a Queen

Wounded

Blood dripping from my veins
Furious
Defiant
Unruly like the tresses flowing down my back
It seems like the harder I fight
The more I resist
The deeper the slices penetrate
Taking layers of myself away before I can yell out

But I dare not surrender
I dare not give up
I dare not give them the satisfaction of hearing my cries
They don't know who they're messing with
The power I come from
The stock I'm made of
The people I'm born of

I have wounds but I'm not wounded
Stained scared and powerless like wimp willows in a
drought
Colored coward in the face of adversity
I am their worst nightmare
An angry scar that won't heal
That won't be quiet because it's too infected

I have wounds but I'm not wounded
I have sorrow but I'm not melancholic
I have wounds
Blood dripping furiously
Angry like the veins that protrude from my limbs
Intolerant

Incapable of closing

I have wounds but I am not wounded
They're reminders that I can conquer
Reminders that I can succeed
Reminders that I can soar above the shallow expectations
placed upon me

I am not their wounded
Their cast away
Their counted out
I am not the one they have power over
I am the power they have yet to discover

I have wounds but I am not wounded
A warrior ready for battle
Bearing the fruits of their self-hate
Pain
Torment and torture
Yet a divine heiress to the kingdom that awaits me

I have wounds
Blood dripping from my veins
Furious
Defiant
Unruly like the tresses flowing down my spine
Flames shining just bright enough to set this all ablaze
I am the one they fear
I am the one they hurt
I am the one they need

Yet I will be the one they lose to
For I have wounds but I am not wounded.

In the Window

I was cookin' at the stove
When baby asked me what my life been like
I chuckled a little bit
That chile always been philosophical
Gleaming into things that seem common sense to most

I started
My life is like me standin' in massa house right now
On the outside
Most would wonder why I'm angry
I don't toil in the sun covered in dirt
My back doesn't feel the sting of the whip
I eat massa leftovers in the quiet of my quarters
To everybody on the outside
My life sparkles
Shines bright with the promise of freedom

But on the inside
Deep down at the core
I'm trapped
My true self drowned in the identity given to me
This isn't the life I dreamt for myself
I imagined my house to be my pit stop
The doors and windows open for whenever my limbs tire
Yet this house is my shackle
Chaining me to a space never meant to contain me

Vibrant hues and the drums of home
That was s'posed to be my life
Freedom
That was s'posed to be my life

I know baby done got lost long time ago
But there's purpose to what I say
Everything ain't what it look like on the outside
My life
To her
Probably is a dreamboat
Masterpiece fashioned by the Almighty

But my life
Ain't nothing but a pendulum swinging
'Tween life and death
Sometimes I visit both for a night or two
Tussle with 'em in my dreams
In my wake
As massa friends stare
As massa touch
As massa wife smack

My life
is
like
a powerful singer with no voice
a graceful dancer with broken legs
a talented window dweller
without a single window to call home
The desire to do
It's there
The capacity to make the leap
Stolen from me like a thief in broad daylight

Father

It's almost sunrise
And as my precious babes play with the angels in their sleep
I find myself with you
Things are hard
I ain't got nothing but scars
A dollar amount on my hands, womb, and back
Children they wouldn't mind trading

But Father
I also got faith in you
Faith that your will can prevail
Faith that my children's children's children
They don't have to suffer the way I am
So Father
I know I call on you plenty
But if you'd just turn your ear to me once more

Dear God
I come humbly to you with shoulders weary
Hands tired
Heart heavy
Like the Israelites slaved under Pharaoh for years
I know I'll be dead before we reap the promise
The promise of redemption
The promise of overcoming

Dear God
I didn't ask for this
Dancing along the sands of my home
Nurturing my future family
That's all I envisioned for myself

But I know all of this is working toward a greater good

Dear God
I pray over the lives of my girls
The Queens who won't have their temples tarnished
My girls who won't be kept in the house
Eye candy to marvel
I pray over the lives of my girls
Who will raise a generation of fearless leaders
The ones who will change the country
The ones who won't give up when it gets tough

I pray over the lives of my girls
The ones who ain't gone care what people say
The ones who gone demand more from their relationships
The ones who ain't gone go for half-done pickings
The ones who will go to war for what's right
I pray over the lives of my girls
They'll be everything I will never have the chance to be

I pray over the lives of my boys
The ones who will be the spine of a nation
The ones who will teach their children
Unafraid of abandoning old rearing customs
I pray they know they can provide more than money
I pray they confess their pains
I pray they confess their wisdom
I pray they hold nothing back

I pray over the lives of my boys
The ones who will become movers and shakers
The ones who will change the world
The ones without the vengeance of massa

Stained onto their backs in the form of lashes
The ones who will open their mouths and not choke

I pray over the lives of my future heirs and heiresses
They have no idea what I endure so they never have to
Lord
Honor me and my cry
Don't let my seeds grow in conquered lands
But allow them to flourish in wild terrain
Unkept and unbothered as they were intended
Father
Something more has to come from me
If I am who you say I am
Then I am protecting the future of gold turned human

Father
Show me my prayers aren't merely breath
Show me that you are a God of your word
Whether you honor me now or while I dance in your courts
Honor me, Father, and set my future up for their greatness

Forgive me of the times I doubt you
Curse you
Throw dirt on your name
'Fore the pain of affliction can be compelling
But in you, I find hope for a new dawning,
Beaming bright

I ask all of these things in your only son's name
Father, please

Ah-men.
Ah-men.
Ah-men.

Ah-

men.

A Cup of Ancestry

The Nadir
The era when racism was worse than any other period after
the Civil War
My soul aches
My eyes can't shed another tear
Those were the words of my ancestors
Lynchings came too close to home
The legal system tightened the noose
It seemed as if having melanin was suicide
In a life where your next breath is too unsure to count on
It seemed as if having a straight backbone ushered death
closer
In a society where they only take power in the form of a
chocolate breath
It seemed as if having fun was a joke
Sundown laws were ruthless
It seemed as if being a Black male made you an automatic
suspect
The burning cross singed the hairs of our dignity, one
injustice at a time
It seemed as if being Black was thrown back into our faces
Confidence in our skin becoming a deeper-rooted evil we
hadn't even anticipated

The Great Migration
The movement of six million African Americans from the
rural South to the urban North
I am tired
I won't continue to be expendable
Those were the words of my ancestor
Break my spirit no more

On our knees, we looked to heavens and searched for the
direction of the North Star
Left in history only to be forgotten, not to lose its power
It still lived
The moss still grew and our natural navigation only
resurrected from within us
Looking towards the babies of this era
We couldn't go on
We needed a breakthrough and to break through
How to release the bondage and preserve a sense of
heritage
The dilemma that troubled the elders for years
Until one said nothing
And the silence spoke volumes
New horizons an unspoken blessing in this bravery
That's it
Bravery
They found the courage Harriet Tubman had
The tenacity of Solomon Northup
The determination of a generation
They found themselves in remembering the past

Break the bones of my ancestors and watch the honey flow
Sweet and fluid as it seeps into my flesh like new morning
dew
It is new morning and day of new mourning
2014
The blood of my brothers flow through the cracks of the
concrete into the hearth of the earth
Weld their blood with my forefathers and be born again in
me
Shining like new money, my armor is royal
I can weather the storm and soothe the cries of a people

I will thrust my rod to the Red Sea
Part the blood of my peers and cross into change
It won't happen this second
It won't happen today
It won't even happen overnight
But when the valleys of freedom
Peace
Serenity
When they are visible
I'll recline in the meadows
Enjoying an overflowing cup of ancestry

Riches to Rags

Often we search desperately for validation from everything
and everyone around us
We want someone to pat us on the back and tell us "good
job"
When we don't even realize that we are richer than the
world could ever be
Didn't you know, you were brought from riches to rags

Adorned beautifully in every color you can think of
I laugh when they tell me my makeup's too bright for a dark
girl
Don't they know, I'm the one to step outside of the
lackluster powders they were playing in
Mesmerized by my reds and golds and blues and hues
They wanted a piece and pleaded desperately
Don't they know, this is a family recipe and they ain't kin to
me

Skin kissed by the sun
I'd like to think I'm a lover in a galaxy full of secret admirers
Do you see how the moon cheekily caresses me in the dark
of the night?
How the sky smiles bright at the sight of me
Don't they know that when you're the royal one, you don't
need to remind anyone

Years and years and years prior to this moment
My grand ancestors smiled, laughed, and shared stories
with the people who'd
Rejoice in the birth of new babies

Celebrate the souls of those who were too big for the Earth
to keep captive anymore
Shriek in pain when royalty no longer meant a thing
Cry when they were punished for no reason beyond being
royal
Suffer torment because they didn't want to surrender
Pray for me to share this space in time in moment in year in
life with you today

I don't know who they think they are when they scoff at my
royalty
Because royalty don't just grow up with a silver, gold,
platinum spoon in their mouths where I come from
Where I grow from
Where I was stolen from
Royalty fight back
Snatch back
Clap back
Royalty be free
Royalty be casual walks in the park with the wind playing
with their curls
Royalty be the cries alone while reading the paper in the
1800s, 1900s, 2000s, forever

See
My royalty way more than they can ever dream of knowing
My royalty you and me and every single person born,
unborn, and born again in between
Don't they know, I was snatched from my throne before I
had to time to know it was mine to keep
Don't they know, I was stolen from riches and thrown into
rags

Don't they know, what they tried to reduce me to was the fuel I needed to plant this seed
Don't they know, I am the Royalty they so desperately want to be.

Stand Up

My beautiful people
Stand up
My eyes are cringing as they take in what you bring to me
This cart of conformity makes me ill with pain
Pain that won't go away until you stop running and make
use of your dormant limbs

My amazing people
Stand up
The look of exhaustion that has overwhelmed your face
frightens me
My heart beats erratically because that look implies you're
on the verge
Teetering on the edge of giving up
Giving up in a world that already placed bets on when and
how far you'd throw the towel in
Don't give them the satisfaction they've stolen from your
insecurity about your power

My wonderful people
Stand up
Your feet that are covered in the blood of the hearts you've
slaughtered
Ripped apart by the pain plaguing you
Us
We
Ripped apart into shreds needed to make us whole again
Stop using your own people as your personal junk yard
A place to salvage the strength that was stolen from you

My people

Stand up
Know that the oh-so-precious faces you carry in your
pocket don't define you
Your temple is priceless so don't mark it down for a bargain
You are of value because of the drum that keeps drumming
Allowing the air to enter and escape
You are of value because of the wisdom in your hair
Sprinkled throughout, leaving a fragrant trail wherever you
go
You are of value because every fabric of your being can't be
standardized
Homogeneity was never destined, only chosen in this
society of constant uniformity

My life giving people
Stand up
Your melanin is a gift
Protecting you from waves of harmful poison meant to
keep you paralyzed
Attack a people meant to keep spreading
Keep living
Keep freeing souls captured in this thought of...
Chill
Fall back
Don't do too much
But I say
Fire up
Empower
Unite
Create a force so numerous that the soldiers bringing up
the rear line the sunset in the hills

My warrior people

Stand up
My talented people
Stand up
My intelligent people
Stand up
My people, my people, my people
Stand up

NAJYA A. WILLIAMS

Part II

What is happening?

~

I pinch myself as a reminder that what I watch on the news, read in the paper, and identify in society is real. When it sinks in that I'm not dreaming and I can't run from this, the pain, anguish, and fear settle deep in my gut. But I don't allow them to stay there. My blood runs too hot and my tongue is too sharp for me to surrender to those feelings.
Ever.

NAJYA A. WILLIAMS

The War on Violence

The War on Violence
Ironic, isn't it?
We are fighting over fighting over fighting, it.
This hidden evil ravaging our society
Our families
Our youth
Our souls
We are battling each other over a war we created
Every word a dagger
Every strike a wrecking ball
Every attempt we make to tear down someone's temple
We devalue our own

What are we accomplishing by carelessly tattooing each
other's walls with permanent ink?
That ink soon bleeds into our souls
Contaminating and infecting our hearts
Causing our body to attack and rid us of the toxin
But the memory remains
Our temples become guarded prisons
Barbed wire edging the 12-foot fence
Watch towers trained on every entrance
Weapons ready to execute any life that dares cross a
threshold

But what lies inside that institution
Is not a wistful princess
Full of ambition, joy, and happiness
A girl with plans that surpass her comprehension
Ideas that will launch her past the light spectrum

Faith that her tiny hands never need to be fisted, for she
has already won
Confidence in her strides because a day never went by
without someone saying
You're beautiful
You're amazing
You never need to put on a soldier's coat
You've won the battle all of us are trying to beat

No, that's not what lies there
This isn't a fairytale
This is truth
What lies there is a crippled soul
Shivering in the cold cell of its former refuge
A slither of sunlight can't be found
The conditions aren't even humane
Constant beating
Constant torture
Constant pain that has yet to be released, let alone healed

Healing
A word never spoken in this place of emotional death
There's no hope
Every remedy has been tested, but has failed miserably
Every medicine
Every drug
Every paralyzer
Every silencer
Every escape
Every distraction
It's useless

Outside, this prison is dull

Lifeless and cold
Like the soul it traps
Our prison system is overcrowded
Too many souls are withering away
We are our own enemy
Carefully picking our counterpart apart
Retaliating against that broken soul who broke them
This must end

Look in the mirror
If no one else says it
You are beautiful
You are handsome
You are amazing
You are royal just because of the unique breath you take
I thank you for your gift
The gift of not being me
Or her
Or him
Or them
Or anybody other than the pure rarity Heaven blessed the
world with
I know you only pick up that weapon
That poison
Because of the pain
Now is the time to let it go
Let that anger go
Let that sadness go
Let that regret go
Let that resentment go
Let that pressure go

Forgiveness

One foot is released
Joy
The other joins its twin
Acceptance
Your arm moves
Contentment
Your arm emerges victorious
Serenity
Your head adorns you
Crystal clear

No more weapons
No more destruction is necessary
No more
Healing has come
Our pain has stopped
That evil that consumed you is defeated
That evil that drove you to hurt no longer hurts you
Beyond saving someone else
You saved the true victim
The face staring at you in the mirror
The War on Violence

The Real Gateway Drug

PAIN
It's a drug found in almost ninety-nine percent of society
today
Quickly entering the body
Its effects still visible years later
Continuing to ravage
Long after initial contact
Consuming every fiber of life
Leaving you stuck in your past
Not allowing you to move on
Live freely
Beautifully
Boldly
Sacredly
Instead you remain high
Your eyes glazed over in remembrance
Silently reliving every haunting detail

But you didn't take this drug willingly
You were poisoned
Given a lethal dosage
With hopes that you wouldn't pull through
But you did
However, the scarring remains
The protective shell you wear
Only gets broken over and over again
Until more poison is seeped into your pores
Soon it takes over your body
Violently distorting your perception
Making you believe that the world is the enemy
Something you must beat in order to not be beaten

That friendly face you used to adore
Now seems to wear an evil mask
Taunting you and causing you more confusion
Everyone becomes the target of the consequences
Consequences of a drug you never wanted in your body
You become numb
No longer acknowledging that everyone has a heart
A soul
A hope
A dream
A desire to be better than the best vision they could paint
of themselves
The blood that lines the streets
The deafening pleas for mercy
The overflowing tears of our broken families
Why are they ignored?

We must eradicate this drug
It destroys too many for it to remain
I beg of you
Let it out
Throw it down the drain
Leave it in the dumpster where it belongs
Because it no longer has a place here
I refuse to let it re-enter my people's palace
For it's only the beginning to the ultimate ending

The Soul of Ferguson

When Mike Brown was slain
I felt the bullet too
We are one in the same
That could've been my blood spilled onto the sidewalk
And it pisses me off because it's royal
It's powerful
It's not meant to be wasted

I see the gardens of old souls
Stones marking each individual fruit that hung from the
trees
Each individual piece of flesh carved from the Black
community's body
One day, I hope flowers mark these spots
Its nectar an open harvest for new beings to enjoy and
continue the reproduction cycle
Rattle my bones and stir within me old spirit
Rain knowledge on me
Save me before it's too late

I knew the end was near when the tanks appeared
Seven-year-old cousins next to me
Middle-aged blue collars next to me
Civil rights era grandmamas next to me
All colors, shapes, and sizes
But our bullet holes the same sizes
I mean, someone come rescue me

Don't stand there with your iPhone tweeting about How
pitiful the situation is
How the world is unrecognizable

How life is unfair because I'm sick of it
Tell me something I haven't heard
Because my ears ain't got the patience for pretend activism
They need petitions
Boycotts
Movements
Powerful expressions of dissent

The soul of Ferguson is on fire
I feel the sting of the tear gas
But milk is nowhere to be found
I feel the pain of my gaping wound
But stitches can't close it
I feel my heart shredding into two
Not because it can't be fixed
Nor because justice just ain't served justly
I feel it ripping to shreds because I'm waiting on that phone
call to come at midnight

When you ask me why I care
I'll tell you that I saw my reflection in the mirror one day
and recognized the bullseye on my chest
When you ask why I hurt
I'll show you pictures of my Afro-Caribbean family, all rich
with melanin
When you ask me why I'm scared
I'll ask you to find the soul of Ferguson for me
When you say you can't find it
I'll say Welcome to Neo Slavery
Soul of Ferguson
Come back to me

Hoodie

I was walking the sleepy streets of my city
with my books and a bottle of water in my hands
But I was seen with a bag of skittles and Arizona can
I walked out the house with a gray hoodie, blue jeans, and
pink sneakers
I was seen with a black hoodie and a sign attached adorned
with the words "Menace 2 Society"
I walked out the house with steely determination to win
today

But the faster I moved to class
The harder the stares felt
The quicker the wind blew
The deeper the assumptions ran
The more I clutched my hoodie to the cold air
The more I felt violated without being touched
I thought their eyes were watching God
But they were really watching me...

Heart beating fast
Heart feeling heavy
I felt an overwhelming amount of grief
In broad daylight
I felt the sting of Zimmerman's accusatory glance in the
faces of those around me
In the glow of the streetlight
He faced the barrel and gunpowder all alone
To Trayvon
My brother, my peer,
My muse
This is for you

Butterflies

I have butterflies rumbling softly in my tummy
I'm at my new school
A place where my skin is exotic
My body a zoo
My language a muse

I own 10 butterflies
All of which live in my body

My first butterfly is excitement
Maybe someone will understand that my name isn't just a name
Or a shoutout to my 'hood
But an ode to my blood and my throne

My second butterfly is curiosity
I just wonder and wonder if someone will take a swab of my skin
Or a strand of my hair
And see if my lies begin there

My third butterfly is happiness
New people, new air
I can be a new me and they wouldn't even know it

My fourth butterfly is pride
A reincarnate of my ancestor
As my tongue is sharper than a razor
Quick like a second
And sugary like the elders' #1 wish:
"Have a blessed day!"

My fifth butterfly is mixed
A hybrid between the cotton-laced land of the South
The cane-filled Caribbean
It isn't the prettiest, but it shines
Skin dark as the cocoa that was once its master
Nose flat as the dreams crushed by burdens and shame
Body as built as the legs keeping me upright when Trayvon,
Rodney, and Fruitvale's son smack me in the face with their
cries

Butterflies six through ten
They never made the cut
Because my truth was too much to digest
My skin too much to see
My words too sharp to hear
My butterflies too diverse
For the U.S. is the land of the free
And the land of the culturally oblivious
An ode to my butterflies

Appropriate

It's amazing to me
Astounding actually
How my blackness has become your platform for
appropriation
Your object of affection and admiration
You have no problem touching my hair
Or staring boldly at my body like you've never been able to
do for your own
Or biting my slang like you poppin enough to come up with
it on your own
Or rolling your hips like you really got the motherland
flowing through your veins

But you really not about this life
Because if you really want my blackness
Take the clenched purses and scared looks I get when I
walk down the street
Take the attacks I face because I'm not the dumb illiterate
everyone wants me to be
Take the catcalls and hungry stares I've gotten on the
street for this body you can't seem to get enough of
Because a hoola-hoop isn't the only thing they want me to
throw in a circle

Take the pain of losing black boys when they're already
endangered
Yeah, they're on the same list as the beloved lions, tigers,
and bears you're more interested in rescuing
Take the pain of reconciling my blackness with my
womanhood to halfway make it in this world
Take it all if you really want it

Don't claim the divinity in my melanin if you can't as easily
accept the ugliness that had to be overcome in my past
Don't claim the good filling of me without acknowledging
the ugly shell you've tried to convince me I live in
Being Black in this society is more than a good twerk, big
lips, and all the other sexualized ideals you've made for me

My Blackness is bold, beautiful, impactful, and
empowering,
These things are very true
But
It also houses darkness, pain, anger, and pure rage
For none of my success came without payment in the form
of suffering.

So take this with you as you go about your day
Appreciation for my Blackness is never an opportunity for
you to use cultural appropriation to glamorize everything
that's beautiful about me
Without acknowledging all you've demonized about me in
the process.

COTTON

Part III

What will happen?

~

The fear of the unknown is crippling.
The fear of the unknown as a woman of
color is strangling. Suffocating. Toxic.
Downright scary. But that fear itself can
kill souls long before the unknown
does. Fight back. Live in faith because
fear can't win. It won't win.
Believe me. We have all that we need
to win. Now, it's time to make it
happen.

Tell Me Why

She was four
He was six
So full of life
So full of energy
So full of positivity
They knew the world was their oyster
Because their momma spoke life into them way before
their first breath

She was ten
He was twelve
The change started to happen
The color of their chocolate skin became a spectacle
School wasn't a joyous occasion when their intelligence
was questioned because the presence of the melanin in
their skin

She was fourteen
He was sixteen
It was then that they had reached adulthood
No longer children in their eyes
Momma and Daddy had to train them on how to walk
without being seen
Huddle close
Don't draw attention to yourself
If you see someone following you, find the nearest spot of
safety
Keep prayed up and faith strong because you never know
when your moment will come

She was sixteen

He was eighteen
It was graduation day
They were filled with so much joy because most of their
friends never survived sixth grade
But that was the moment of self-destruction
Because the second they embraced that they'd survived all
those years
Bullets went flying and the manifestations of their
greatness was cut short
So please tell me why I should bring light into this darkness
when my candle is a target

Tell me why I should bring life into this world when others
are seeding plants of death for them
Tell me why
Why should I move forward
Why should I keep going
Why should I bring little chocolate drops into this world
when cocoa is under attack

Tell me why
I should take a chance and have a part of me brave the
storm I'm so desperately trying to escape
Tell me why my future heirs should have inheritance at
stake
Because just as soon as they emerge from darkness
Extinguishers are waiting to put of the flames I've stoked
for nine months within me
So please tell me why
I should train my children up to be prepared for death

Tell me why

I should train my children to choose their lives before
attempting to save me
Tell me why
I should want to bring children into a world that aims to
destroy me
Tell me why
I should want to birth a future King and Queen into this
world
When I'm not sure they'll make it home to their castle every
evening
Tell me why
I shouldn't be afraid of the possibility that I may have to
bury them before they bury me

Prince

I am scared
Quite terrified of what's been done to the male species
I watch in anguish as the melanin that once symbolized
beauty morphed into a national symbol of weakness
My tears flow through their hearts
Attempting desperately to fill in the gaps left by the terrors
of life

Why has my baby boy become a target?
They are trying to murder my son
The media coaches him to look like a thug
Hollywood socialites and mainstream entertainers
encourage him to act like a thug
And when members of society clutch their belongings a
little tighter when he passes by
I cry harder
My baby boy is a statistic in the making
"Daddy, when will you be out of the courtroom today?"
The most disturbing question I've ever heard a little boy ask
a grown up

What is happening to my little black boys?
Why are we replacing books and educational flash cards
with game consoles and toy guns?
Then expect them to behave as well trained mutes when
they become teenagers
We are raising our boys not to become men
But just another horror story on the five o'clock news
Baby boy, no one will ever tell you what I'm about to tell
you
Please listen to me

I'm trying to save your life
And I'm gonna do that with five simple rules

Rule number one
When society proclaims you are a thug, look around in
confusion
Tell them your name and its meaning because thug ain't
what ya mama named you and surely didn't raise you to be
so don't let the world try to make you into one

Rule number two
Wear your dignity and pride like a crown on your head
The moment you bow in submission
And allow your crown to fall carelessly to the ground
You'll fit the description of every suspect before you even
say your name

Rule number three
Don't cover your smile. Be proud of your pearly teeth and
the happiness that encouraged you to smile
When everyone else mean mugs the world, be the one to
find beauty in the possibilities life offers
Just because everyone houses melancholy doesn't mean
you have to go visit them

Rule number four
Protect your right to be a young, intelligent, Black boy.
You are just as worthy as any other human to be here
Don't let negativity blow away the cloud carrying you to
success

Rule number five
Don't ever stop dreaming

We often tell our young girls to dream but boys must be
men with realistic goals
Life's too short to be unhappy
Look up to the sky and speak what you want
The atmosphere listens, collects, and ushers you closer to
your destiny then you'll ever know

Remember, this Queen appreciates you
This Queen knows the importance of a young, handsome
brown skinned boy
You are my Prince who will become a King
I love you now and I'll love you forever
Proud to stand by your side and hold your hand, I can't wait
to see you blossom
Be strong, void of fear, and make me proud
To my one and only
Prince

Princess

Women are beautiful creatures
Elegant and graceful
Maternal and loving
Sophisticated and powerful
Seemingly the glue of life
Women are special
We are dependable and trustworthy
Always there and on time no matter the occasion

We are consistent
I mean, just look at our make up
But this seems to be an archaic perspective
Women are not pillars anymore
Instead, we search aimlessly for pillars to lean on
We are dying at the hands of our own

See, way back when Sunday dinner was a thing
Grandma never cooked alone
She had this child picking greens
This one cutting onions
Crying to death like they do every year
And that sweet-spirited baby trying their best to set the
table
Grandma had support beams holding her up like the
beautiful fortress she was
Grandma demanded respect by her presence
Just a stern look was enough to straighten out the most
hard-headed little one
No one stepped out of line

Grandma had priority seating on public transportation and assistance with her groceries
She was a sight to see on Sunday mornings
Her hat lain gracefully on her wispy coils and her suit fitted unlike any other
A Mother of the church, her cheek was adorned with many kisses by the end of service
Grandma had the community backing her no matter what

What has happened to the respect we had for our women?
Now, our women are nothing more than an object of affection
An object to be used and disposed of when society is done with the "new marvel"
But listen to me, baby girl, please listen to me
You were always a marvel
The day I held you in my arms, I knew a diamond was born
I knew the world was blessed a thousand times over
You know why?
Because you have billions of individual and unique pieces that make you special
I love everything about you and know that in your body, mind, and soul

Don't wait on a man to tell you your worth
Don't wait on a friend to tell you you're awesome
Don't wait on society to tell you you're drop-dead gorgeous
Don't wait!
Because the minute you buy into their stock claims of adoration
You've already lost the investment you have in your personal happiness
Listen to mommy, don't be average

NAJYA A. WILLIAMS

Don't succumb to the wills of the world
It's beyond being politically correct, it's about surviving
It's not always about what you know, it's about who you know
And that one you spoke death into could've spoke life into you
Don't misrepresent what you stand for
You were raised to stand on your own two feet and fight for your wealth
Not lie down and take what's tossed to you
When that elderly woman comes on the bus, give up your seat
Tell her thank you for paving a way for me to be able to sit where I want to sit
Princess, life is so much bigger than your body
What the world wants to use and abuse you for
Go and explore the abundance but heed my warnings
Know your femininity and embrace it
Know your power as a young Queen
Don't try to fill my stilettos
Make your own and start a new brand

And if I don't tell you enough,
I'm so proud of you in the present that I become ecstatic at the thought of your Queendom in the future
I love you until the ends of this earth
Go make me proud and grow into your essence, beautiful child
My baby, my heart, my reason for living
My Princess

This is for my Sisters

Dear sister
I know it's been a while since we last spoke
And the only reason I reached out is because it's time for a
heart to heart
I see the pain etched across your face and exhaustion
floating in the brown orbs you call eyes
I see it, sis, and I'm so sorry I neglected your cries
Because while we were fighting feverishly for our
endangered brothers
You were drowning in their shadows
Reduced only to the narrative of Sandra
Leaving your reality as an afterthought when the dust has
cleared

Dear sister
I know you're tired
The burden of carrying life
Saving life
Giving life
Serving life
Offering life
Being life
Is a lot to bear
But I'm begging you to put the cape down because if you
look at your priority list
Are you even on it?

Dear sister
I pray for you each and every day
And I'm not sure if you're religious or not

But the craziness of today's time makes me drop to my
knees in pleading to God for mercy
Because our bodies are being exploited
Palaces defiled with spray paint graffiti
Stained black and blue
Riddled with damage
Bloodied canvases distorted beyond recognition
I'm in tears because as long as you rock a miniskirt, high
heels, and little makeup
They'll always say that you begged for it

Dear sister
I just want you to love you for you
So many people demand that you love them purely and
without relenting
Destroying yourself piece by piece to build them up
But I dare you to demand a fierce, unapologetic love
Because you are deserving
But it'll never come if you don't believe it for yourself
Let's be real
I know you love Beyoncé
But you are already in Formation

Dear sister
I want you to know that I'm rooting for you
We often run this race of who has the most bundles, beat
face, and nicest figure
But I don't care about all that
I just wanna see you happy and winning
Keep me going by giving me an example to aspire to
Know above all else that I am secure enough in myself to
root loudly for you
Because sisterhood is more than a relationship

It is a dynamic pairing of souls who are ready to change the
world because of, not in spite of, each other

Dear sister
I love you
And I'm sorry that I even had to write this letter to you
With all of the focus on rescuing our Black men,
understanding our intersectionality and place in the
feminist movement, and building kingdoms
We forgot to pour back into ourselves
But I challenge you to fall back in love with yourself
Fight desperately for the face you see in the mirror daily
and never let her go again
For she is worth far more than earthly riches

Dear sister
I am proud of you
And I can't wait to see how you shine once you leave this
galaxy as a shooting star in exchange for a new home in
your career, philanthropy, service, innovation, and even
your future little shooting stars

Brotha

Black Brotha, I love ya, I will never - try to hurt ya
I want ya, to know that, I'm here for you - forever true
Black Brotha, strong brotha, there is no - one above ya
I want ya, to know that, I'm here for you - forever true

Angie Stone did me justice as a Black woman when she
wrote this song
I've grown up surrounded by a plethora of Black men
Lovingly doting on me and rooting for me when the rest of
the world didn't know that they should do so too
I can't even explain what it means to see a Black man and
be able to love on him
As his sister, homie, lover, friend

In a lot of ways, Black men are synonymous with an
endangered species
Except the press only started to cover a problem that's
existed for decades upon decades recently
I pray for them because just as much as Black women glue
the community together, Black men carry it on their backs

It's hard to be a woman of color on this campus
It's hard to be a woman of color in this country
It's hard to be a woman of color in this world
It's hard to exist in this society
But Black men, they make it worthwhile

They make the late nights and working twice as hard to get
half as much concept worth enduring
To know that society will know them beyond Dr. King's,
Trayvon's, and Mike's tragic narratives

To know my future children will see kings and leaders who
look just like them

To all the Black men in this room
Thank you
Thank you for holding me accountable to you
Thanks for learning how to be accountable to me
Thank you for affirming me as a light when I feel drowned
by darkness
Thank you for loving on me
Thank you for sharpening me
Thank you for leading me
Thank you for allowing me to lead you
Thank you teaching and being taught
Thank you for not being complacent in the ordinary
Most importantly, thank you for being you, radically and
unapologetically

There's nothing more inspiring than watching you step into
what you were called to do without pause

To the Black men in this room
I'm gonna keep fighting for you
I'm gonna keep expecting your best in all you do
I'm gonna keep wanting you to just simply be you
I care for you
I cry for you
I laugh with you
I dance with you
I grow with you
I pray for you
I carry you
I love you

I love you
I love you
And I'll tell everyone I know
No matter the circumstances
Cuz you're my

Black Brotha, I love ya, I will never - try to hurt ya
I want ya, to know that, I'm here for you - forever true
Black Brotha, strong brotha, there is no - one above ya
I want ya, to know that, I'm here for you - forever true

Tongue

It's the day after the election
And it feels as if my tongue has been ripped from my mouth
I can't breathe
I
cannot
breathe.
Inhaling as if a weight is lying comfortably on my ribcage
I can't breathe
I can't form words
My mind is a land of mush

An avid advocate for those unheard
I feel the same fear they do
These times seem all too familiar
I walk outside and await the dogs
Sit at the counter and await the hot coffee and slurs
Walk to class and await the not-so-subtle aggressions
All this time
America thought that Jim Crow was assassinated in 1964
When he just hid underground until he was called upon
again
Having tea and cupcakes with his father Slavery
Breaking bread with his nephew Mass Incarceration

See
I'm nervous
The moment we use the voice our ancestors cultivated
We are chopped down til there aren't any of us left
What can I say
Who can I talk to
How can I advocate

NAJYA A. WILLIAMS

Marching and yelling on the frontlines is who I am
Yet instead of empathetic faces watching from the side
I have rifles and evil incarnates waiting to end me
What do I do when it seems that activism
The one space where change is created
Could land me in a cell or the grave
Long before I see the fruit of my labor

I imagine this how my slave ancestors felt
Silenced
Rid of their tongue
Not because they didn't know how to fight
They felt trapped between saving their future children
And keeping the living ones safe
Because then and especially now
Speaking out comes at a price

If I shout too loud,
A bounty is placed on my head
And the collateral damage will always involve family
They don't want any remnant of me to come back
Loud, bold, and unapologetic again

If my slave folk ran too fast
Ran too far
All the slaves were beaten
Tortured and punished so they knew never to try it
And don't let the fugitive lose their fight
Seeing their bloodied, decaying flesh is persuasive
If I want my family alive,
I must stay subservient

So what do I do
It's the day after the election
And as much as I want to tweet
As much as I want to fight back
I'm afraid of the backlash
The metaphorical stripes cast against me
No job, no education, no livelihood
Just death and the constant looking over my shoulder
Because I've outed myself as intolerant

It's the day after the election
and
it
feels
like
my
tongue
has
been
torn
from
my
mouth.
I can't breathe
I can't speak
I can't be what I need to be

And
truthfully
that's what hurts the most.

Beauty

Beauty
An idea that has yet to be truly defined in this society
A society that shouts loud and clear
Ricocheting off the walls of our lives
You'll never be enough
You aren't unique
You'll never be someone worth a second, let alone a minute
A minute of time time so precious that you've become
merely mediocre
But why subject yourself to these fallacies
These ideas you accepted as truth knowing they're far from
it

Why?
It's easier, huh?
What would the nation look like if everything was "easy"?
Sojourner Truth could have chosen ease
But the cries and pain of her people told her otherwise
Rosa Parks could have chosen ease
But the aching, soles of her weary feet yelled to her
I'm tired of conforming for someone else's ease
Fight for your comfort
Martin Luther King, Jr. could have chosen ease
But the power that propelled him beyond his pulpit
couldn't be ignored
Why choose ease?
Acceptance?
Conformity in a life that isn't meant to be average

If it were, would we have a need for things like race or
gender or belief systems?

We are beautiful
Shocking, I know.
You are beautiful
Why, you ask me.
Why not?
You are beautiful because of that unique heartbeat that
serenades you every morning
You are beautiful because of the air you breathe
Taking in the world and giving back a piece of you
You are beautiful because you look nothing like the person
you're next to
You are because you are able to challenge that one fact I
thought I knew

You are beautiful
We are beautiful
From our skin to our smiles
Size to our shape
Beliefs to our ideas
We epitomize beauty
And I know this is hard to accept
But it's true
You're so confused by this because you're blinded
Blinded by hatred, racism, discrimination
Pain from the person who dripped these lethal drugs into
your veins like an IV
No dialysis can get rid of them
Only the acceptance and acknowledgement of your beauty
can cure this disease

We must move from poison to persistence
Persistence in making sure the person next to us knows
that they are a special patch needed in this quilt

A quilt woven by the hands of our forefathers who knew
beauty isn't the body we are stored in
But the soul that runs through it
We are beauty
On the road to recovery
Travelling away from the land that captured you in the idea
that you're ugly
Not worthy of beauty even caressing your face
But you glow more than your skin ever could
You reach depths your eyes can never discover
You reach heights your legs will never carry you
Physically, you are just a messenger
But you are beautiful
We are beautiful
Our unique bodies mesh together to make an abstract so
beautiful
Only a true connoisseur could appreciate

Come together
Grab my hand
Grab her hand
Grab his hand
Grab any hand snatched away by the fear of recognizing
their own power
Come together and make a profound statement
A statement not many will ever hear
We are beauty

Dream Us Free

I remember it like it was yesterday
The most captivating dream took hostage my mind
It felt as if my dreaming psyche subdued me
Forcing me to just sit and listen

The elders used to always tell me that we have two ears
And one mouth
For a reason
God gave us a hint and we just don't take it

So
I obeyed Him
Eyes wide open
Ears wide open
Mouth closed shut
I wasn't going to miss this moment

This dream
It was like any other
I saw my grandchildren
Playing in the sand on the beach
Just as chocolatey as ever

I was in a cabana with their ma and pa
Watching closely like the mama bear I was born to be
Their squeals of joy made my lips curve up
Rewarding them a smile they didn't need to earn

Hours and hours went by
'Fore we finally packed up and headed home
See

This where the dream gets strange
My conscious mind soon identified the city as Money
And quickly tried to cry out
But my dreaming psyche stilled me
And forced me to keep watching and listening

My baby driving
The radio on
And in the dream
I stay stone still in the back seat
Unable to move while watching my grandbabies sleep

As if the universe knew how hard I was praying us safe
I heard the sirens
And immediately
My heart began to race

Pulling over,
My baby wakes everyone and forces them to put their
hands up
The police officer came
And
They
Reached
In
Their
Waistband

I was just sure that "Murdered Family of Five"
That'd become our posthumous identity
Quietly obeying my baby
I keep watching and listening

When the officer brings his hand back into to view
All I can see is a notepad
A pen
A warning
A "slow down and have a good day"

Not a gun
Not a gun
Not a gun
Not a gun
Not a gun
Not a gun

It was not
A
Gun

That's my dream
To not have a panic attack in the car when I see sirens
To not have a panic attack when a cop stops me
To not have a panic attack when my family is sought
To not have a panic attack when a badge is made visible

That's my dream
To not have to dream about this
To not have to hope my PD protects me
And
Not
Kill me

That's my dream
To wake up and not want to hold my family captive
Trapped in a bubble of prayer and holy oil

All because the world has colored their skin demon

Lord, that's my dream
That's my dream
That's my dream
That's my dream

And as I sit here,
With tears in my eyes
Tremors in my hands
And despair in my heart

I can only dream that it'd come true
I can only dream that it's God's will
I can only dream that this isn't a cruel, cosmic joke

I can only dream
Us
Free.

NAJYA A. WILLIAMS

~

Acknowledgements

Immense gratitude for my heavenly Father, as I couldn't have done it without Him; my mama, for being the woman I strive to be; papa, for showing me what I come from and what I can touch in this world if I remain true; my nuclear family, for encouraging me to nurture and develop my gift; Pavita Singh for her phenomenal editorial services; Hakeem Angulu, for the design of my imprint logo; Phyllis Ryder, for her immeasurable commitment to my work and journey as a woman of color; Wanda Jones-Hinnant, for her leadership of the SWW Poetry Club and her unwavering support; Kip Smith, for all the times he gave me the support and good laughs I didn't know I needed; my testifiers, for all of the wondrous ways they made me blush. Their words were like sweet honey melted in my ears; *The Fam*; my Harvard family for cheering me on every step of the way.

Special thanks to my friends, far and wide, for motivating me to keep writing and performing; my extended family and network for your continued support.

It takes a village, and they certainly ushered me closer to my dreams.

NAJYA A. WILLIAMS

COTTON

Reading Group Discussion Questions

Poetry + Spoken Word

1. What role has poetry played in your life?
2. Do you think poetry is a lost art? Why or why not?
3. Who is your favorite poet? How did you encounter them?
4. If you had to describe a moment that changed your life in a poem, how would you go about doing it? Would it be easy? Difficult?

Give it a try:

_____
_____
_____
_____
_____
_____
_____
_____
_____
_____
_____
_____
_____
_____
_____
_____
_____
_____
_____
_____
_____
_____

87

Family

1. Is family important to you? Why or why not?
2. Can people whom you are not related to serve as your family? If so, how can those connections positively or negatively impact your relationships with your biological family?
3. How can one promote healthy relationships within their family?
4. How do you advocate for members in your family, including yourself?
5. What do familial/ancestral ties look like to you? Why do they matter?

Mental Health in the Black Community

1. Do you think that mental health is discussed enough in the Black community?
2. How can we promote mental wellness in everyday life?

List a few ways here:

_____
_____
_____
_____
_____
_____

3. How has mental health, wellness, or illness impacted you and/or your family?
4. Given the tragic events that we see often in the news, how can we better cope while remaining active and

engaged social activists?

Social Activism and Art

1. Can art serve as a means to inciting social change?

2. If you had to choose, what form of art would you use to encourage sociopolitical change? Why did you make this choice?

3. What do think artists can teach social activists and vice versa? Do you think that artists are required to discuss social activist themes in their works?

4. Can one person effectively navigate life as a social activist and artist? What would it mean if the person ever had to betray one purpose for the sake of preserving the integrity of the other?

NAJYA A. WILLIAMS

Stay Connected

Born and raised in Washington, D.C., Najya Williams is an undergraduate at Harvard College in Cambridge, MA. She aims to pursue a career in Pediatric and Neonatal Medicine. A youth advocate and social activist, Najya has committed to participating in numerous poetry- and spoken word- driven events to shed light on issues present in her community that many consider taboo. She was recently recognized by The Harvard Foundation and The Black Men's Forum for the work she has cultivated and continues to maintain within the Black community on Harvard's campus. Najya looks ahead to continue making a difference in not only her community, but in the nation as a whole, one word at a time.

Follow Najya's work as a scholar, writer, and activist via:
Twitter: @NajyaTheAuthor   Instagram: @NajyaTheAuthor
SoundCloud: "The Invitation" by Najya
Website: najyawilliams.com

NAJYA A. WILLIAMS

COTTON

NAJYA A. WILLIAMS

COTTON

NAJYA A. WILLIAMS

www.ingramcontent.com/pod-product-compliance
Lightning Source LLC
Chambersburg PA
CBHW020554030426
42337CB00013B/1092